The Universe and Multiple Reality

The Universe and Multiple Reality

A Physical Explanation for Manifesting,
Magick and Miracles

M. R. Franks

iUniverse, Inc.
New York Lincoln Shanghai

The Universe and Multiple Reality
A Physical Explanation for Manifesting, Magick and Miracles

iUniverse, Inc.

For information address:
iUniverse, Inc.
2021 Pine Lake Road, Suite 100
Lincoln, NE 68512
www.iuniverse.com

ISBN: 0-595-29472-3

Printed in the United States of America

This book is dedicated to Edwin Hubble—the astronomer for whom the Hubble Telescope is named—the man who truly discovered that there is a universe out there. He was a lawyer.

This book is also dedicated to Marie Laveau, who never quite understood why her rituals worked.

Contents

1

Postulate One

Every conceivable energy state exists.

There is no one reality. Each of us lives in a separate universe. That's not speaking metaphorically. This is the hypothesis of the stark nature of reality suggested by recent developments in quantum physics. Reality in a dynamic universe is non-objective. Consciousness is the only reality.

The purpose of this short book is to suggest a model for quantum superposition of realities, the better to visualize how these quantum effects "leak out" into the macroworld and indeed define it.

This first postulate simply asks us to assume that every possible arrangement of matter and energy consistent with the laws of quantum physics exists. This postulate asks us to assume, among other things, that a universe exists "right now" somewhere that differs from our own only in that one electron on one remote planet of one distant star in, say, the Andromeda Galaxy is in a less excited energy state. Another universe exists that differs from the present universe only in that one photon, of all the photons in the room where this book is being read, is positioned exactly one Ångström unit to the left. Another universe exists in which the earth has two natural moons. Another universe exists in which there is no planet earth. Another exists in which Elizabeth Taylor has brown eyes. Another exists in which George Washington has a wart on his nose.

If a universe can be imagined, it exists. Nature abhors a vacuum and fills that "vacuum" with every conceivable universe.

The late Sir James Jeans, the great British astronomer, was among the first scientists to recognize the universe as a creature of imagination. He wrote in 1932:

> To-day there is a wide measure of agreement, which on the physical side of science approaches almost to unanimity, that the stream of knowledge is heading towards a non-mechanical reality; the universe begins to look more like a great thought than like a great machine. Mind no longer appears as an accidental intruder into the realm of matter; we are beginning to suspect that we ought rather to hail it as the creator and governor of the realm of matter—not of course our individual minds, but the mind in which the atoms out of which our individual minds have grown exist as thoughts.[1]

This new knowledge compels us to revise our hasty first impression that we had stumbled into a universe which either did not concern itself with life or was actively hostile to life.

Indeed, every conceivable arrangement of matter and energy, however improbable, is postulated to exist as a separate universe.

These universes are, however, static—not dynamic. Dynamic concepts of energy and of motion and of time and of change with time have not yet been introduced into this discussion. While every conceivable arrangement of quarks, gluons, subatomic particles, atoms, molecules, photons and energy that could possibly be imagined is assumed to exist, this first postulate asks us only to assume that each such arrangement exists in a frozen state for all eternity. Each of these imagined universes is eternally like an ice palace or like a still frame in a reel of motion picture footage. The frame exists forever simply because it is capable of being imagined, and because nature abhors a vacuum.

This suggestion is not entirely strange to quantum cosmology. Hugh Everett first postulated "parallel universes" in 1957. David Deutsch, a research fellow at the Department of Astrophysics, Oxford, and a professor at the University of Texas, tells us:

I think it's safe to say that there is a very large, probably infinite, number of these universes. Many of them are very different from ours, but some of them differ only in some minute detail like the position of a book on a table, and are identical in every other respect.[2]

Paul C. W. Davies and J. R. Brown tell us:

If the many-universes theory were correct, however, the seemingly contrived organization of the cosmos would be no mystery. We could safely assume that all possible arrangements of matter and energy are represented somewhere among the infinite ensemble of universes. Only in a minute proportion of the total would things be arranged so precisely that living organisms, hence observers, arise. Consequently, it is only that very atypical fraction that ever get observed. In short, our universe is remarkable because we have selected it by our own existence![3]

Notice, however, that while Everett, DeWitt, Deutsch and others postulate an infinity of universes, each of their postulated universes is dynamic, moving, changing. Bryce DeWitt of the University of Texas tells us that under this theory "every quantum transition taking place on every star, in every galaxy, in every remote corner of the universe is splitting our local world into myriads of copies of itself. Here is schizophrenia with a vengeance!"

There can be no doubt that these pioneers envision multiple worlds that are dynamic, moving and changing.

P. C. W. Davies and J. R. Brown speak of the imaginary experiment involving Schrödinger's cat, so named for the physicist Erwin Schrödinger, who first conjured up the idea in 1935. In this thought experiment a cat is placed in a box. A quantum event determines whether this imaginary cat is poisoned or not. Perhaps a Geiger counter is arranged to count the number of particles encountered in a defined time period, and if the count is odd, a hammer is tripped and a glass vial's deadly contents are inflicted on the cat. If the count is even, the cat is allowed to live. However the situation may be arranged, it is arranged so that a quantum event determines the cat's fate.

Quantum physics tells us that upon the happening of the event the cat goes into two superimposed states, one of being half alive and the other of being half dead. Only when the human experimenter arrives later to look into the box does objective reality "collapse" in upon the events. And then that reality instantly collapses back retroactively to the time of the fateful event. Speaking of this, Davies and Brown tell us:

> According to Everett the transition occurs because the universe splits into two copies, one containing a live cat and the other a dead cat. Both universes contain one copy of the experimenter too, each of whom thinks he is unique. In general, if a quantum system is in a superposition of, say, n quantum states, then, on measurement, the universe will split into n copies. In most cases, n is infinite. Hence we must accept that there are actually an infinity of 'parallel worlds' co-existing alongside the one we see at any instant. Moreover, there are an infinity of individuals, more or less identical with each of us, inhabiting these worlds. It is a bizarre thought.[4]

In Everett's view, because each of these worlds is dynamic, the live cat goes on living in the one world, while in the other world someone presumably takes the carcass out of the box and buries it.

David Deutsch tells us that Everett's universes all are "changing in content."[5]

The present postulate differs from their thinking in that here each of the postulated universes is absolutely static, frozen, unchanging.

2

Postulate Two

*Starting at any imagined energy state, there will be an infinite number of
imagined energy states that differ from the starting energy state by one and only
one quantum transition, and a larger, transfinite number of energy states that
differ from the starting energy state by more than one quantum transition.*

The term "energy state" is used synonymously with "imagined static
universe"—one static permutation or one conceivable arrangement of
all the energy in the universe. An energy state or static universe that
differs from another by just one quantum transition (for example, by
the energy level of one electron attached to one atom) would be in the
first category. An energy state or static universe that differs from
another more radically (for example, by Elizabeth Taylor's eyes being
brown) would be in the latter category, as many billions of atoms are
involved in the color change.

A brief discussion of the two-slit experiment is here in order. An
article in the *Christian Science Monitor* said it succinctly:

> Through the ages, the nature of light has puzzled researchers. Most
> 18th-century physicists, including Newton, held that light was cor-
> puscular—composed of tiny particles. Early in the 20th century
> that idea was reconfirmed by experiments showing that light con-
> sists of quanta of energy now called photons. Photons, it appeared,
> could knock electrons off atoms—acting somewhat like softballs
> hurled at dolls in a fairground tent. Moreover, you can count single
> photons as they strike a sensitized plate. So light, it seems, behaves
> like pellets shot from a gun.[6]

Back in 1803, however, Thomas Young, a London physician and physicist, proved something else about light: It was also made of waves. His proof was based on the fact that when two separate wave patterns overlap, they don't simply blend, like different colors of paint. Instead, they produce something known as an interference pattern.

There's nothing mysterious about that pattern. It appears, for example, whenever you drop two stones close together in a pond. Knowing this, Young set up his famous two-slit experiment.

Light from a point source is passed through a card or other opaque material containing two parallel slits, landing on a wall or screen on the other side. If light were particles, one would expect the image of the two slits to project on the wall. If light were waves, one would expect an "interference pattern" of alternating bright and dark lines.

The astounding result of the experiment is that one gets an interference pattern even if the photons are released one at a time! A single photon should be able to go through only one of the two slits. Yet it appears that a photon going through one of the slits "knows" of the existence of the other slit. The so-called Copenhagen Interpretation of quantum theory—so named because its originator, Niels Bohr, was a professor at the University of Copenhagen in the 1920s—teaches that each photon takes all possible paths simultaneously, and that it is only by observation that one of those paths is "frozen" into reality! Pascual Jordan, one of the founders of the Copenhagen Interpretation, tells us that "the electron is forced to a decision. We compel it to assume a definite position; previously it was, in general, neither here nor there."[7]

An article in *The Economist* tells us:

> Taken at face value, quantum mechanics appears to say some rather odd things about the universe:
>
> • There are no such things as "things". Objects are ghostly, with no definite properties (such as position or mass) until they are measured. The properties exist in a twilight state of "superposition" until then.

- All particles are waves, and waves are particles, appearing as one or the other depending on what sort of measurement is being performed.

- A particle moving between two points travels all possible paths between them simultaneously.

- Particles that are millions of miles apart can affect each other instantaneously.[8]

Under this postulate, each possible path of the electron represents a series of energy states. Each of these states exists in objective reality. An energy state or static universe that differs from another by just one route taken by one of the photons encountering the two slits would be "contiguous" to the starting energy state. But an energy state or static universe that differs from another more radically would be non-contiguous. *(non-contiguous = touching)*

3

Postulate Three

All imagined energy states can be ordered.

The postulated energy states or universes can be placed in an order, much as are words in a classic thesaurus or colors on a color wheel.

I will call this ordered structure the "superuniverse," borrowing a term from *The Urantia Book,* but giving it an entirely different meaning. I shall not use the term "multiverse," so popular in quantum physics, for the reason that their multiverse is seen as consisting of multiple dynamic universes with no particular structure being specified. Here, the term I use refers to an orderly lattice or structure of static universes.

Let us now arbitrarily define energy states, static universes, as either "contiguous" or "noncontiguous." Two energy states that differ from one another by only one quantum transition are deemed contiguous. Two energy states that differ by more than one quantum transition are deemed noncontiguous.

The number of energy states contiguous to any given energy state approaches infinity. Each of these contiguous energy states is in turn contiguous to other possible energy states that differ from it by just one quantum transition.

All possible energy states are thus placed in a multi-dimensional lattice. It may be helpful to think of a sheet of paper filled with hexagons drawn such that each hexagon is contiguous to six other hexagons. A tile floor made of hexagonal tiles illustrates in two dimensions a set of such contiguous "universes."

If we go from this two-dimensional analogy to a three-dimensional one, it is easy to imagine a bubble-making machine blowing bubbles of

contiguous = touching

equal size into a container. Each bubble standing alone would, of course, be a sphere. But pressed against the adjacent bubbles on all sides, with no intervening space or gaps, each bubble must share its walls with the adjoining bubbles and each bubble therefore takes sides in the form of planes. Polyhedra spontaneously form.

Several types of polyhedra, in fact, may be useful as analogies. Cubes nest solidly with other cubes, such that each cube is bounded by six others, with no space wasted. Twelve-sided rhombic dodecahedra will nest solidly with other rhombic dodecahedra, such that each dodecahedron is bounded by twelve others. Truncated octahedra likewise nest solidly with no gaps, and each shares fourteen faces with its fourteen neighbors. Another geometric solid, the hexagonal cylinder, can be so arranged that each has as many as twenty identical contiguous neighbors.

As we increase the number of dimensions in our analogy, we find the number of available sides and contiguous interfaces increases. David Bohm feels that at the superholographic level the universe may have 10^{89} dimensions, as many dimensions as there are subatomic particles in our three-dimensional universe.[9]

It may well be that we can assume even more dimensions, since most every quantum event has innumerable possible outcomes. When an electron and a positron annihilate, for example, the resulting photon may head off in virtually an infinite number of directions. The one photon represents not just one dimension but a googolplex[10] of dimensions, one for each possible path and each possible polarization it could take exiting the annihilated pair. Accordingly, each particle in the universe represents innumerable possible transitions, and each of these possibilities is in fact a separate universe.

To comprehend the magnitude of this, some discussion of the concept of "googol" and "googolplex" seems warranted. The terms were introduced by Edward Kasner and James R. Newman in their classic 1940 book, *Mathematics and the Imagination*. The authors tell us:

It is a fair inference that kindergarten children can enjoy lectures on graduate mathematics as long as the mathematical concepts are clearly presented.

It was raining and the children were asked how many raindrops would fall on New York. The highest answer was 100. They had never counted higher than 100 and what they meant to imply when they used that number was merely something very, very big—as big as they could imagine. They were asked how many raindrops hit the roof, and how many hit New York, and how many single raindrops hit all of New York in 24 hours. They soon got a notion of the bigness of these numbers even though they did not know the symbols for them. They were certain in a little while that the number of raindrops was a great deal bigger than a hundred. They were asked to think of the number of grains of sand on the beach at Coney Island and decided that the number of grains of sand and the number of raindrops were about the same. But the important thing is that they realized that the number was finite, not infinite. In this respect they showed their distinct superiority over many scientists who to this day use the word infinite when they mean some big number, like a billion billion....

...The number of atoms in the average thimble is a good deal larger [than the number of grains of sand on Coney Island beach]. It would be represented by perhaps 100000000000000000000000000000. The number of electrons, in size exceedingly smaller than the atoms, is much more enormous. The number of electrons which pass through the filament of an ordinary fifty-watt electric lamp in a minute equals the number of drops of water that flow over Niagara Falls in a century.

One may calculate the number of electrons, not only in the average room, but over the whole earth, and out through the stars, the Milky Way, and all the nebulae. The reason for giving all these examples of very large numbers is to emphasize the fact that no matter how large the collection to be counted, a finite number will do the trick....

...Words of wisdom are spoken by children at least as often as by scientists. The name "googol" was invented by a child (Dr. Kasner's nine-year-old nephew) who was asked to think up a name for a very big number, namely, 1 with a hundred zeros after it. He was very certain that this number was not infinite, and therefore equally certain that it had to have a name. At the same time that he suggested "googol" he gave a name for a still larger number: "Googolplex." A googolplex is much larger than a googol, but it is still finite, as the inventor of the name was quick to point out. It was first suggested that a googolplex should be 1, followed by writing zeros until you got tired. This is a description of what would happen if one actually tried to write a googolplex, but different people get tired at different times and it would never do to have Carnera a better mathematician than Dr. Einstein, simply because he had more endurance. The googolplex then, is a specific finite number, with so many zeros after the 1 that the number of zeros is a googol. A googolplex is much bigger than a googol, much bigger even than a googol times a googol. A googol times a googol would be 1 with 200 zeros, whereas a googolplex is 1 with a googol of zeros. You will get some idea of the size of this very large but finite number from the fact that there would not be enough room to write it, if you went to the farthest star, touring all the nebulae and putting down zeros every inch of the way.[11]

Yet if we are ultraconservative and assume just one dimension for each of the 10^{89} particles in the universe, the number of hyperfaces to each hyperpolyhedron in our model still staggers the imagination.

The problem is similar to that of sphere-packing. It seems fairly settled that a sphere can have no more than 12 identical spheres placed adjacent to it in a three-dimensional lattice. (If polyhedra or geometric solids are used instead of spheres, as discussed above, the number is slightly greater.) In either case, as the number of dimensions increases, so does the "kissing number," the number of spheres contiguous to a given sphere. By the time one reaches just 24 dimensions, the number of spheres contiguous to a given sphere is 196,560.[12] Operating in 10^{89} dimensions or more, the number of universes contiguous to any one given universe would exceed a googolplex.

Perhaps the leading authorities on sphere packing are John H. Conway and Neil J. A. Sloane. Professor Conway teaches mathematics at Princeton University, while Neil Sloane works at AT&T's Shannon

Lab in Florham Park, New Jersey. (Mathematical models for sphere packing are useful in calculating the number of telephone conversations that can be carried simultaneously on a wire, fiber or microwave channel.[13]) Conway and Sloane have written a book that includes an algebra for sphere packing in a space of an infinite number of dimensions.[14]

It is impossible for our human minds to picture a hypersphere (a sphere of more than three dimensions) or a hyperpolyhedron (a polyhedron of more than three dimensions). Our minds function in three dimensions of space, and our ability to visualize seems limited to those three dimensions.

At what point would one "contiguous" universe touch another? At all points in space! Let us reason by analogy. Hexagons are two-dimensional figures in two-dimensional space. Contiguous hexagons touch along an edge. Thus, two-dimensional figures touch along a one-dimensional line. Rhombic dodecahedra or truncated octahedra are three-dimensional figures in three-dimensional space. Contiguous geometric solids touch along faces. Thus, three-dimensional figures touch in two dimensions. N-dimensional figures touch in (n-1) dimensions.

Hyperpolyhedra of 10^{89+} dimensions would be contiguous in far more than just our three familiar dimensions. Every point in three-dimensional space—every molecule on earth out to the farthest galaxy, would be "contiguous" to the next universe, touching it at every point! We would not consciously perceive these contiguous universes as such because we as humans are capable of perceiving just three spatial dimensions at a time. Our minds, however, can and do in fact move from contiguous universe to contiguous universe as shall be explained.

To imagine these "contiguous" universes from our limited perspective, picture these shadowy universes as virtually superimposed on one another.

No mention has been made of time as a "fourth dimension," or of "spacetime" as an entity. Time will re-enter this discussion shortly, but not as a dimension. Albert Einstein taught that time is the fourth dimension, and Hermann Minkowski suggested that space and time are indistinguishable from one another. Recall Minkowski's famous quotation:

> The views of space and time which I wish to lay before you have sprung from the soil of experimental physics, and therein lies their strength. They are radical. Henceforth space by itself, and time by itself, are doomed to fade away into mere shadows, and only a kind of union of the two will preserve an independent reality.[15]

While their insight was brilliant, and while "world lines" and "light cones" have their usefulness, it may well be that it is inappropriate to think of time as a true dimension, or as anything other than a subjective experience. More reflective of the modern approach is the thinking of Henryk Skolimowski, professor of philosophy at the University of Michigan. He writes:

> The mind is one of the lasting mysteries of the universe. It is not the slayer of the real, as some Hindu traditions maintain. It is the creator of the real. Whatever we know, we know through the agency of the mind. The mystery of the mind is thus doubly profound: not only is it an extraordinary creation of nature—exquisite and puzzling in its own right; it is also the shaper and creator of reality. On the way the mind works depends the nature of our knowledge, and (a step further) the shape of the external world. What the mind cannot render, the world cannot bear. And what the world bears is exactly what the mind renders....

> ...We are now at an altogether different juncture. What we need is not an update of Einstein but a different model of reality, and a new theory of the mind. This is then our program—to create a new model of the mind that truly makes sense of this participatory universe and our role in it. Needless to say, we want to create a theory both rational and coherent. Yet this rationality must not be at the mercy of the criteria of mechanistic rationality, which is a peculiar product of empiricism and a guardian of its conceptual universe.[16]

The ability of mind to influence matter at a distance, and over eons of time, is perhaps best illustrated by the "gravitational lens effect." In space, a quasar, a brilliant source of light very distant, can lie directly behind and in the same line of sight as an intervening galaxy. Rather than the nearer galaxy blocking the view of the more distant quasar as one might expect, the gravitational field of the intervening galaxy acts as a sort of "lens," bending the light so the quasar directly behind it can be seen. The quasar, however, appears in multiple images, above, below and to the sides of the intervening galaxy! The intervening galaxy, of course, is massive, and has a diameter of at least 100,000 light years.[17] Depending on how the observing equipment is set up on earth, the incoming light behaves exactly like waves passing around the intervening galaxy on all sides, or like particles each of which takes a definite route to one side of the intervening galaxy or another. John Wheeler says:

> But the new feature about the delayed choice version of this experiment is that we can wait until the light or photon (that is going to activate one of the counters) has accomplished almost all of its travel before we actually choose between the photon going by both routes or a photon going by only one of the two routes....
> ...The photons reaching us start out more than five billion years ago—that is, before there was anyone on Earth. Waiting here on Earth we can today cast a die and at the very last minute decide whether we will observe an interference photon (that is a photon which has come, as we jokingly describe, 'both ways') or change our method of registration so that we will find out which way the photon has come. And yet the photon has already accomplished most of its travel by the time we make this decision. So this is delayed choice with a vengeance![18]

Yet if a human mind today can influence the route or routes taken by a photon as it left its quasar five billion years ago, how much easier is it for that mind to influence the course of an electron at the synapse in the brain? Yet in each case, as well as in Alain Aspect's experiment to be discussed, the question in reality is not one of whether the human mind can influence the route taken by a photon (or in the case of the Aspect experiment, the polarity of a photon). The question is rather into which still "frame" the consciousness of the observer will enter, taking that frame as it is, including its representation of events that "happened" eons ago!

The present writer's model of reality does not treat time as a "dimension" in any way. This author feels that time can no longer be thought of as "just another dimension."

By this third postulate we have now put every imaginable universe into an ordered latticework of all imaginable static universes. We'll call this the superuniverse, distinguishing it from the multiverse of conventional quantum physics. This superuniverse too is static, unchanging, eternal. All imaginable energy states are represented, and all are interconnected by a contiguity that envisions one quantum change at a time.

4

Postulate Four

Mind or spirit exists independently of the physical brain.

Paraphrasing Descartes, I think, therefore I am a spirit. My consciousness is the one phenomenon secular humanism cannot explain.[19] Materialism can explain the evolution of my body and brain. It can even explain much of my behavior—why unthinking matter-in-motion would act as if it had a conscious mind as well as an unconscious mind: A "bicameral mind" has survival value.

Julian Jaynes of Princeton theorized in 1976 that man initially evolved to have a "bicameral mind," *i.e.,* a compartmentalized mind with an "executive part" and a "follower part." Jaynes then postulated that consciousness somehow evolved out of the breakdown of this bicameral mind. He gave no credence to any mind apart from the physical matter-in-motion of the brain: "Somewhere here in a mere three-and-a-half pound lump of pinkish-gray matter, the answer has to be."[20]

But the fact that something has survival value does not explain how it came into being, much less how it operates. Assume arguendo that there would be survival value in man's teeth being made of industrial-strength diamonds rather than of calcium. That feature's excellent survival value alone could never have caused *homo sapiens* to evolve to have diamond teeth. Diamonds can be synthesized only in high-pressure blast furnaces, it must be remembered, and furnaces are singularly lacking in the embryonic environment.

It's a long leap from saying that some feature has survival value to explaining how that feature could ever hope to evolve from available materials and existing processes. To say that man should behave as if he were conscious sheds little light on how consciousness operates or by what process consciousness "evolved" out of thin air. Like diamond teeth in a living being, consciousness invites a better explanation of how it got there and how it operates.

Surely a mindless computer could be programmed to act as if it had feelings and an awareness of its own existence. But that fact and the computer's ostensible behavior do nothing to explain my actual feelings and my very real awareness of my own existence. I don't just act as if I feel; I feel, and I know I feel. I have a spirit, and the fact that that may have survival value explains nothing of what my spirit is, where it came from, or how it operates.

Jaynes's thinking is typical of the school of philosophy known as materialism. Materialism is but one of several schools of thought. Professor Subhash Kak of Louisiana State University explains:

> Countermodels to materialism begin with the argument that as ordinary matter does not appear to have self-awareness, a machine like man should not have it unless it had an existence of its own. This belief in a mind which is more than an epiphenomenon raises several difficult issues of its own. For instance: What is the seat of the mind in the body? Does the mind outlast the body? Does an overmind, a consciousness, pervade the universe of which the individual minds are the temporarily separated fragments? Does the mind enter the body at conception or does it emerge out of the developed body later? Can mind influence matter? and so on. The suggestion that the mind exists as a subtle body inside the brain has often been made. This represents man as a machine with the mind dwelling within him as a pilot. In another view matter is perceived to be a mere figment of the mind, which makes it hard to explain the observed regularity and commonality of the physical world. To conclude, then, several views exist with regard to the mind-body problem. Some of these are:

1. Materialism: Mind is a record of sensory impressions. Consciousness is a by-product of certain complex neural events and it first emerged at some state in phylogeny.

2. Panpsychism: Mind is associated with all matter as an inherent attribute. It is reflected as sentience or consciousness in the higher animals.

3. Dualism: Both mind and matter have independent existence and consciousness is a reflection of the mind on the body. The material world is causally closed.

4. Monism: The fundamental entity of the universe is consciousness. It is not known how the physical universe springs from this entity. Nevertheless, to understand the universe one needs to understand consciousness.[21]

The currently fashionable view may be described as "functionalist." Mind is looked upon as software. Among the leading functionalists are Douglas Hofstadter, Paul C. W. Davies and Karl Pribram. Davies and Hofstadter see consciousness as the product of a "strange loop" between different levels of structure,[22] while Pribram posits a holographic model for the mind and brain.[23]

Karl Pribram, a neurophysiologist at Stanford University, sees consciousness as a hologram. Pribram claims that memories are not stored in any specific location in the brain. They appear to be distributed over the whole brain, much as any portion of a holographic image is distributed over the whole film.

True, there are certain special places in the brain that control certain special functions—centers or specific places for vision, centers or specific places for speech, et cetera. Talbot tells us that an early American psychologist, Karl Spencer Lashley (1890-1958), whom Talbot claims was a neurophysiologist, discovered back in the 1920s that damage to any one specific portion of the brain interfered with the functioning of the sense that that one part of the brain specifically controlled. However, Lashley later learned that higher-level brain functions, including memories and the ability to remember, were not destroyed.

Lashley is the originator of the school of thought known as *antilocalisationism*. In his research, Lashley would teach animals to perform tasks and then destroy a specific area in the animal's brain. Lashley then noted the effects. He found that all cortical areas can substitute for each other and that the reduction in learning is proportional to the amount of brain destroyed. Lashley's name is also associated with phrenology, the semi-occult practice of "reading" bumps on one's scalp or skull much as a practitioner of palmistry "reads" lines on one's palms.

To further consider the holographic model, when a portion of a photographic film containing a holographic image is destroyed, no portion of the hologram that that film produces is destroyed. Instead, the entire image is simply weakened or made fainter. Talbot tells us that many neurophysiologists now take the fact that memories are not destroyed when a part of the brain is damaged as proving that the functions of memory are not located in any specific place in the brain, "but are distributed over the brain as a whole in much the same way that the image of a hologram is enfolded in all of its parts."[24]

Sir John Eccles is a dualist who won a Nobel Prize in 1963 for his work on the synapse. He believes mind or spirit is separate and distinct from the physical machine called the brain. He believes man has an immortal soul.[25]

Mind is postulated to exist independently of the physical brain. As we shall see in another context, the brain may be a mere "tuning mechanism" to receive the non-local mind, much as a radio receiver is a tuning mechanism to receive non-local signals.

I think, therefore I am. My spirit exists.

Either I am the only spirit in this universe, or other spirits also exist. If other spirits also exist, they abound. Surely I cannot be the greatest of these. My spirit, therefore, is testimony to the existence of a greater spirit than mine. My awareness of my own existence is all the proof I need of the existence of a higher power.

5

Postulate Five

Existence consists of sequentially experiencing contiguous energy states.

It is here postulated that all sentient consciousness exists independently of any one physical universe, and moves from contiguous energy state to contiguous energy state at quantum speed, lingering in each universe for only a "jiffy," the smallest imaginable quantum unit of time, 10^{-43} seconds, being that fraction of a second represented by the number 1 over the number 10 followed by 42 zeros. Doing so, the sentient being experiences the illusion of a continuous existence in one dynamic universe with quantum interactions taking place, all in accordance with the laws of physics.

We're talking about the mind, soul or spirit moving through literally ten trillion trillion quintillion energy states per second. Perceived reality consists of this "movie" made up of an incredible number of still frames selected on a mix-and-match basis. A time line for a "mind" moving on a route through contiguous universes would thus look like a random and meandering line drawn on a floor made of hexagonal tiles, where each tile represents a separate contiguous universe.

The pioneers of the many-worlds hypothesis do not see it this way. Just as they envision multiple worlds that are dynamic and not static, so too do they envision multiple consciousnesses. Paul Davies tells us:

> Not only our bodies, but our brains and, presumably, our consciousness is being repeatedly multiplied, each copy becoming a

21

thinking, feeling human being inhabiting another universe much like the one we see around us.

The idea of one's own body and consciousness being split into billions upon billions of copies is somewhat startling to say the least, yet the proponents of this theory have argued that the splitting process is quite unobservable, because the replicated consciousness cannot communicate in any way with its siblings. In fact, the separate worlds of superspace are all completely disconnected from each other as far as communication is concerned....

...So what starts out at birth as one consciousness multiplies countless billionfolds by death.[26]

David Deutsch writes in *The Fabric of Reality* that "each copy of us can directly perceive only one universe."[27]

Wheeler also envisages the multiple splitting of consciousness itself. Wheeler, Everett and DeWitt are brilliant scientists who deserve much credit for the many-universes hypothesis and the idea of a superuniverse—they call it the multiverse. It is easy to understand their view that reality consists of a multiplicity of dynamic universes, and they ought not be faulted for the greatness of what they did achieve. It is easy to understand their blindness to the obvious possibility that parallel universes are static, that time and motion are but illusions, and that it is mind traversing the frames in rapid sequence that gives rise to perceived reality and to time and motion itself.

What seems apparent, that consciousness moves through a labyrinth of static universes, is perhaps more difficult for the scientific mind to accept than for the general public. These scientists are the same people who for years accepted only the tenets of materialism, thinking more in terms of "brain" than "mind" and virtually denying the existence of "mind" altogether. Consciousness, we were told, is a transitory phenomenon, a "strange loop" of the brain that probably dies when the body dies. No immortality here.

Michael Talbot uses these words:

The standard answer of science is, of course, that there is no ultimate distinction between mind and body. Consciousness is synonymous with the brain, and when the brain dies all of those things that we associate with consciousness—self-awareness, perception, acts of understanding, and so on—die with it. The opposing point of view is that we are more than the sum of our parts and when we die some aspect of our consciousness survives and goes on. If we accept this point of view, the question then becomes, What is the something that survives?[28]

So science, believing what Talbot describes as the standard answer and not the opposing point of view, was left with no choice when faced with irrefutable evidence that an event does not have meaning unless observed. Since each parallel universe contains a physical near-copy of the observer, science was forced to conclude that his consciousness must split too!

Yet instinctively we know this is wrong. I am aware of myself in one continuous thread of existence, and I find it difficult to imagine that my consciousness is dividing itself untold thousands of times each second. Either I would be aware of the division of myself, or my consciousness is favoring one of the branches over the other. The latter, of course, is the closer approximation of truth: my consciousness indeed is taking just one of the "branches." And the other branch, not having a thread of consciousness running through it, is nothing but a collection of empty, dark, static universes and truly not a branch at all. These are "failed universes" for me, but only for me, and only because my consciousness failed to enter them.

What will be the reaction of followers of Everett, DeWitt, Wheeler, and Davies when they realize that it is indeed consciousness that moves through a series of static universes, rather than dynamic universes themselves splitting and consciousness splitting with the splitting universes? We must assume that as scientists they will welcome this additional insight and refinement of their original, bold concepts.

Stephen Hawking asks us in another context:

What should you do when you find you have made a mistake like that? Some people never admit that they are wrong and continue to find new, and often mutually inconsistent, arguments to support their case—as Eddington did in opposing black hole theory. Others claim to have never really supported the incorrect view in the first place or, if they did, it was only to show that it was inconsistent. It seems to me much better and less confusing if you admit in print that you were wrong. A good example of this was Einstein, who called the cosmological constant, which he introduced when he was trying to make a static model of the universe, the biggest mistake of his life.[29]

Fred Hoyle, one of the last century's great astronomers, came a brave and honest long way from the essentially atheistic steady-state theory he co-authored in 1948 with Hermann Bondi and Thomas Gold.[30] His 1948 "steady state" theory, so popular in the 1960s, was intended primarily as an alternative to the "big bang" hypothesis. Contrast that with the same Fred Hoyle's 1983 suggestion that the evidence now shows the universe to have been structured by intelligence! After suggesting that interstellar particles are bacteria, Hoyle then said:

This sets the stage for the origin of life on the largest conceivable stage. The stage is not local, not restricted to our solar system nor even to our own galaxy, but truly cosmic. If an intelligence was involved in the origin of life, the intelligence was very big indeed, as I suspect is recognized by the religious instinct residing in all of us, the instinct that whispers in some remote region of our consciousness. Life is therefore a cosmological phenomenon, perhaps the most fundamental aspect of the Universe itself.[31]

Hoyle goes on to postulate that the principal feature of the universe is an abundance of life virtually everywhere—even in space—and that the universe has intelligence. Curiously, Jean E. Charon, a theoretical physicist at the University of Paris, in his seminal work on unifying all four physical interactions (the gravitational force, the electromagnetic force, the strong nuclear force, and the weak nuclear force) posited that all matter has consciousness. Every atomic particle exists in hidden dimensions in its own imaginary microuniverse, has consciousness, and appears holographically as a point in our own universe, according to Charon.[32]

The idea of an intelligent universe directing events is not limited to Hoyle and Charon. Rupert Sheldrake has proposed some radical ideas on this, according to Talbot.

Sheldrake posits that there exists a force or field connecting all members of any species, including those in the past. Sheldrake claims that each species of animal, humans included, have a "group mind" that he claims may explain certain psychic phenomena. Talbot claims that when nature does something, that event causes nature to want to repeat the event and the more the event is regurgitated, the stronger the "M-field" becomes.

Talbot also reports that Sheldrake claims living organisms are not the only things controlled by M-fields. There is a strange phenomenon that exists in the field of crystallography that Talbot claims can be accounted for by Sheldrake's M-field hypothesis: when a newly invented chemical substance crystallizes, it takes a long time for crystals to form. It is as if the new chemical is indecisive as to what form it should crystallize into. Finally, the substance decides the form of its crystals. From then on, *all over the world, crystals of that substance form quickly in that same shape.*

Talbot reports that a 1961 book, *Crystals and Crystal Growing,* by Alan Holden and Phylis Singer, tells of an event that happened in the early 1950s at a company trying to grow large crystals of a chemical known as ethylene diamine tartrate. After three years of research, the company still could not develop a monohydrate form of the substance in crystalline form. On the other hand, the company knew that the anhydrous form of the chemical was easy to make, and they went with that variety instead. The anhydrous crystals they produced were then sold to another company for use in industrial applications.

Talbot tells us that a year later, the crystals in the growing tanks suddenly started coming out in misshaped form. *The company then found that these "misshaped" crystals were actually the very monohydrate form they had been trying so hard to produce a year earlier.* Additionally, this new crystalline form then began appearing elsewhere, even at other factories.

Talbot claims that "because of the frequency with which this phenomenon occurs, Holden and Singer go so far as to suggest that different planets possess different dominant crystal forms."[33]

There is wonder in a snowflake, grown high in some stratus cloud one molecule at a time. How does a molecule of water attaching itself to one of the snowflake's six arms "know" precisely where and how to attach itself so as to keep symmetry with five other arms, each located trillions of molecules away? The snowflake, it would seem, demonstrates the presence of a cosmic consciousness, a non-local mind.

The thinking over the past forty years has changed. First we believed in one dynamic universe that has always been here, uncreated and unchanging, the ultimate manifestation of Sir Charles Lyall's uniformitarianist dogma that nothing ever really changes, a universe in which man is regarded as matter in motion. From that we went next to a "big bang" model of one unique, dynamic, changing universe that was supposedly created, or perhaps just happened into existence, about fifteen billion years ago, and in which mind and consciousness are explained in functional terms.

Today science is beginning to accept spirituality. Edgar Morin, director of research for the National Center for Scientific Research in Paris, expresses it this way:

> From this point on, while the materialists continue to call the mind an epiphenomenon, the spiritually oriented people try to conceive of the brain as a sort of network that captures "transmaterial" messages which are transmitted in a psychic or information field. The brain does not "produce" the mind but "detects" it. The information that penetrates the senses "materializes" itself in chemical sub-

stances and neuronal changes, which register physically the symbolic meaning of sensory perceptions.

These spiritual conceptions, forced to compromise with the material reality of the brain, result in a collaborative dualism or interaction, which accepts the fact that spiritual reality requires the cooperation of a material reality to carry out its work.

This spiritual resistance on the mind-brain front is bolstered by a reversal in the situation where materialism had won its most decisive victory, that is, in the basis of physical reality. The collapse of material substantiality at the subatomic level gave rise to an enigma and a mystery, and there spirituality rushed in, hoping to reconquer the world not in spite of, but due to the progress of science....

...The brain cannot explain the mind; furthermore, it needs the mind to explain itself. Thus the brain cannot conceive a brain except via the mind, which itself cannot conceive a mind except via the brain.[34]

Now at last we are on the brink of accepting that we live in a superuniverse, that this superuniverse is static and unchanging, and that consciousness constitutes the only reality. This superuniverse may always have been here, or it may have been created, or it may simply exist in a supermind. In any case it is timeless: the big bang is tomorrow for the mind that chooses and is able to explore those particular frames. Time is no longer a fourth dimension. In a universe of an infinite number of dimensions, time is the subjective and individualized sequencing of an observer's visits on his unique route through individual static universes.

Writer Talbot puts it thus:

[I]t may be that consciousness, like the quantum, does not possess any single and precise location at all. Sometimes it seems to be inside our heads. Sometimes, via the infinite interconnectedness of the quantum landscape, it seems to [go elsewhere, as in clairvoyance or astral projection]. But in truth it never "goes" anywhere at all. It simply accesses whatever perspective on the universe it wants via the nonlocal realm from which it operates.[35]

Alain Aspect, of l'Institut d'Optique Theorique et Appliquée in Orsay, France, conducted the definitive experiment that leads us to this conclusion. Certain types of atoms can emit two photons simultaneously, which then travel away from each other in opposite directions at the speed of light. The photons are polarized. That is, as they travel they have a particular angular orientation that may be horizontal, vertical, or any angle in between. If we think of light as waves, imagine horizontally-vibrating waves or vertically-vibrating waves or waves vibrating in any plane in between. As we all know, polarized light can be "screened out" or "screened in" with polarized filters. (This principle and the fact that most sun glare is polarized are the reasons polarized sunglasses are effective to screen out glare.)

When an atom emits two photons simultaneously, the polarity of the two photons is correlated. Strangely, if the polarity of one of the photons is altered by being passed through a series of filters, the other photon always responds by adopting the identical polarization! This is true even though the two particles are traveling away from one another at the speed of light. Conceivably, the two photons could have been traveling apart for thousands or millions or even billions of years, emitted eons ago by a distant galaxy! It is clear that any two photons so emitted simultaneously remain eternally in communication with one another over great distances and great time periods.

What Aspect wanted to find out was whether the communication between such a pair of photons is superluminal (that is, faster than light). Atoms were caused to emit twin photons of light that sped apart with identical polarization. Aspect devised a method to test the polarity of the photons at their respective finish lines. It was known that altering the polarity of one of the photons by passing it through a polarizing filter altered the polarity of the other. What was not known was whether the change in the second photon occurred instantaneously, that is at a speed faster than the speed of light.

The experiment was conducted in France in 1982—and the findings have shaken science and cosmology to the very core. The team of physicists (his Groupe d'Optique Atomique—the Atomic Optical Group) also included Jean Dalibard, and Gérard Roger of l'Institut d'Optique Theorique et Appliquée de l'Université de Paris Sud (the Institute of Theoretical and Applied Optics of the University of Paris South) in Orsay, France—just outside of Paris. Aspect published the results of the experiment in a short, three-page paper in *Physics Review Letters,* entitled "Experimental Tests of Realistic Local Theories via Bell's Theorem." The results of this crucial experiment proved one of two things: either objective reality simply does not exist beyond the mind of the observer, or faster-than-light communication—meaning communication with the past and future—is theoretically and actually possible.

Science writer Michael Talbot finds it surprising that an experiment of such import would virtually be ignored by the media and the public. Talbot says that the implications of the experiment "are so profound they seem more science fiction than science fact.... [T]he conclusions of the Aspect experiment are unequivocal. These are not hypothetical assertions. At least one of the above two options must now be accepted as fact."[36]

The Aspect experiment essentially proves the mathematical proof known as Bell's Theorem. The late John Stewart Bell, the Belfast-born senior theoretical physicist for CERN in Geneva, Switzerland, proved that under quantum theory either the world is nonobjective and does not exist in one definite state or it is "non-local" and action-at-a-distance is instantaneous.

Of course, in the Aspect experiment no "action at a distance" has really occurred, and the simplest explanation is that on altering the polarity of the first photon the mind of the observer has simply entered a series of universes or still frames consistent with that new polarization. The distant photon in this frame has the identical polarity, of course.

Yet even the conscious mind's motion through the lattice of universes is not without some limitation. Some directionality of motion through the lattice is necessary here, corresponding to the arrow of time. One doesn't experience heavy objects falling from the ground into the sky or heat flowing from cool into warm objects contrary to the entropic mandate of Clausius's Second Law of Thermodynamics. One would experience such perceptions were the conscious human mind able to move freely "backwards" through the frames. But consciousness apparently is not free to move haphazardly through the lattice, but seems to be "pushed" through. This push is the force we think of as "time," and this unseen force usually compels us to move through the lattice primarily in one general direction (from one or more "past" frames to one or more "future" frames). Still, there is great room for variable paths, as every quantum event is a fork in the road at which the mind still can go in any one of several different "future" directions.

The Causal Order Postulate states that for Event A to cause Event B, Event A must come earlier in time than Event B. The Causal Order Postulate was not in Einstein's original Theory of Relativity. Einstein added it to please his critics! And the Causal Order Postulate has effectively been demolished by the Aspect experiment and its progeny. Causation *can* move backwards in time. Later events can effect earlier events.

An age-old question also has been answered: If a tree falls in the forest and no one is there to hear it fall, is there a sound? The answer must be no, since dynamic reality consists only of perceiving. Until there is a perceiver, we have merely a dead collection of adjacent frames. They would need to be seen sequentially, as one might view a cinema, for an event to "happen." These frames are capable of being viewed in a different order. Some of them might be traversed by a mind moving through the lattice on a different route, such that the outcome of the event is entirely different.

It is the passing of the conscious mind through particular frames in a particular sequence that gives vitality to the event represented by those frames. Existence is a movie, the staccato-like frames of which are quantum jumps. Vitality and action are illusions subjectively experienced by the conscious mind viewing the movie.

Sitting in the film can, Tara doesn't burn and Clark Gable doesn't talk. It's just a collection of dead still frames called *Gone With the Wind* until those frames are brought to life by being viewed in a particular order by a conscious mind.

The tree in the forest exists in trillions of trillions of quintillions of still frames, each differing from the others by one or more quantum transitions. But in this absolute reality there is no falling of the tree, no sound of the tree falling, no chirping of the bird. A conscious mind must move through the latticework of adjacent universes in a particular sequence to perceive a motion of the tree, and if those moves are made on a particular path through the latticework the tree will be perceived to fall and to make a sound.

Einstein once asked, "Surely the moon exists whether or not somebody is looking at it?" Truly it does, but it reflects no light. Static photons frozen in space for all eternity do not move anywhere. It is only by the mind moving through the frames rapidly that the photons appear to move. The movie then comes to life and there is light.

Motion, energy and time are but the illusions of perceiving one still, frozen universe after another. No wonder on the microscopic scale everything moves in quantum jerks and jumps.

6

Postulate Six

Each conscious being's trail through the lattice is unique to that being.

Each conscious being may have his own route through the latticework, experiencing his own unique dynamic universe and experiencing events different from the events other conscious beings experience as they move on slightly or radically different trails through the lattice-work.

Any one human mind perceives other human beings that seem to move, talk, and feel according to the laws of physics, but these other beings may or may not be inhabited by conscious minds. It is impossible to tell whether another human is merely "matter in motion," a veritable android conforming to an atheistic or materialistic model, or a sentient being inhabited by a conscious mind.

We thus return to the solipsism of old—nothing exists beyond my own immediate experience—but with a new twist: each other person being observed may or may not be sentient, or may today be inhabited by a sentient mind whose trail may diverge from my own tomorrow, leaving me to perceive a non-sentient android that moves according to the laws of physics from frame to frame and that I think to be still sentient.

Yet day after tomorrow, the trail of the sentient mind formerly inhabiting that android may once again return,[37] and its consciousness and mine may again track relatively parallel paths through the lattice for a time. Time lines for two minds moving through the same frames and sharing the same reality, then diverging, and then returning to a shared reality, would look like two meandering lines drawn on a hexagonal tiled floor that join their paths at times and diverge at other times.

Jorge Luis Borges said it well in his collection of short stories, *Ficciones*. He tells the story of a fictitious book:

> Before I discovered this letter, I kept asking myself how a book could be infinite. I could not imagine any other than a cyclic volume, circular. A volume whose last page would be the same as the first and so have the possibility of continuing indefinitely. I recalled, too, the night in the middle of *The Thousand and One Nights* when Queen Scheherezade, through a magical mistake on the part of her copyist, started to tell the story of *The Thousand and One Nights*, with the risk of again arriving at the night upon which she will relate it, and thus on to infinity. I also imagined a Platonic hereditary work, passed on from father to son, to which each individual would add a new chapter or correct, with pious care, the work of his elders.
>
> These conjectures gave me amusement, but none seemed to have the remotest application to the contradictory chapters of Ts'ui Pên. At this point, I was sent from Oxford the manuscript you have just seen.
>
> Naturally, my attention was caught by the sentence, 'I leave to various future times, but not to all, my garden of forking paths.' I had no sooner read this, than I understood *The Garden of Forking Paths* was the chaotic novel itself. The phrase 'to various future times, but not to all' suggested the image of bifurcating in time, not in space. Rereading the whole work confirmed this theory. In all fiction, when a man is faced with alternatives he chooses one at the expense of the others. In the almost unfathomable Ts'ui Pên, he chooses—simultaneously—all of them. He thus creates various futures, various times which start others that will in their turn branch out and bifurcate in other times. This is the cause of the contradictions in the novel.
>
> ...*The Garden of Forking Paths* is a picture, incomplete yet not false, of the universe as Ts'ui Pên conceived it to be. Differing from Newton and Schopenhauer...[he] did not think of time as absolute and uniform. He believed in an infinite series of times, in a dizzily growing, ever spreading network of diverging, converging and par-

allel times. This web of time—the strands of which approach one another, bifurcate, intersect or ignore each other through the centuries—embraces every possibility. We do not exist in most of them. In some you exist and not I, while in others I do, and you do not, and in yet others both of us exist. In this one, in which chance has favored me, you have come to my gate. In another, you, crossing the garden have found me dead. In yet another, I say these words, but am an error, a phantom....

...Time is forever dividing itself toward innumerable futures and in one of them I am your enemy.[38]

There is no one dynamic, changing universe; rather, each conscious being has his own personal dynamic universe. Time is the illusion experienced by sequentially visiting contiguous energy states. At each quantum event the universe does not split into parallel universes. (Strictly speaking, "contiguous" universes would be perpendicular to three-dimensional space as we know it. "Parallel universes" is a misnomer.) Rather, consciousness merely enters one of numerous contiguous static universes.

This concept contrasts with the ideas of Everett, DeWitt and others who first postulated the "Many Universes Theory" or the theory of "Parallel Universes." In their original concept, the universe actually divides into two copies of itself at every quantum transaction. Each observer divides, and presumably is conscious, real and moving in each division. Each copy of this observer after being so divided is unaware of the other.

Many-universe advocates agree that it is equally plausible for Everett's "branching" to work backward in time as well as forward. Thus, in their view, different universes from the past are constantly fusing into the present.

An excellent example of such fusing of multiple pasts into a changing present, of altering history as it were by weaving different paths from the past into one changed present, is the excellent film *Frequency*,[39] which starred Dennis Quaid and Jim Caviezel. Past events can be altered.

Hollywood rarely gets the science right in "time warp" movies. This time, however, Hollywood hit the quantum nail right on the head. Nothing that happened in *Frequency* is theoretically impossible. Just as Schrödinger's cat can divide and take multiple paths into the future, multiple strands from different pasts can weave into one present.

Such "fusion" of different universes from the past might explain why different individuals coming to a transaction sometimes have radically different memories of the "same" past event.

From the outside, the superuniverse looks like a multidimensional version of our "packed polyhedra" or "packed spheres" model.

But since we humans cannot imagine more than three dimensions, we know only how this labyrinth looks from the inside, from our earthbound viewpoint. If we slow the footage down so as to view the frames one jiffy at a time, at any instant it is as if each of zillions of contiguous universes are superimposed on the present universe, all the way from the room in which I now sit to the farthest star.

Each of these contiguous universes differs from the universe I am presently visiting (for a jiffy) by just one quantum transition. Universes more than one quantum event away are not contiguous. But in a jiffy my spirit will enter one of these contiguous universes, at which time a whole new set of zillions of universes will become contiguous to my new temporary abode. The universe I have just left will, of course, be one of these. But most of the other universes contiguous to it have now departed and are no longer contiguous to the new universe I have just entered. And in a jiffy this process will repeat itself.

7

Postulate Seven

The path one's consciousness takes through the lattice
is determined by multiple factors.

Movement of a mind through the lattice appears to be in part directed from outside, in part directed by the imagination of the mind itself, and in part directed by a collective affinity of mind for mind.

I am conscious and yet I did not choose to enter the superuniverse at my present position; or if I did I am certainly not aware of my having done so. It follows either that the present position of my consciousness in the superuniverse is a chance event or that I was "put here" by some other consciousness or force.

Forces external to the mind seem to act upon the mind to "push" it along in a particular direction. The first of these forces acting on the human mind is the general entropic push from "past" to "future." A second external force, a God, may also direct a mind in a particular direction, sometimes seemingly working a miracle in the process. Divine or spiritual intervention would explain how so many of us have met near death on so many occasions, particularly as children, but we're not dead yet. It is almost as if a hand of divinity intervenes on behalf of persons, particularly children, sparing them from many of their close calls with accidental death.

The individual mind itself has some control over its movement through the lattice. It has long been a tenet of the occult that man is indeed created in God's image in the sense that every thought is an act of creation, tending to manifest in the physical world that which is first imagined. Only now is it beginning to be recognized in the sciences that "mind over matter" may have a basis in fact.

John Archibald Wheeler tells us:

> The universe does not exist "out there" independent of us. We are inescapably involved in bringing about that which appears to be happening. We are not only observers. We are participators. In some strange sense this is a participatory universe.[40]

And the late veteran British cosmologist Fred Hoyle tells us:

> It is a strange aspect of science that until now it has kept consciousness firmly out of any discussions of the material world. Yet it is with our consciousness that we think and make observations, and it seems surprising that there should be no interaction between the world of mind and matter. Instead of picturing ourselves as external observers, quantum mechanics seems to imply that we cannot separate ourselves from the events that we are observing, sometimes to the extent of actually determining what takes place.
>
> In learning about quantum mechanics students are usually told that, because "macro-events"—those in everyday life—involve such a large number of atoms, they are determined by a vast number of individual quantum mechanical occurrences, and therefore depend only on statistical averages which can be calculated with complete certainty. Macro-events are represented as being completely predictable, whereas the micro-events that make them up are not. But this separation seems quite arbitrary.[41]

The human mind tends to track through the latticework in the general direction of a physical frame or energy state imagined first. Thus, imagination even by a human mind may be thought of as an act of creation tending to "cause" the realization of that which is first imagined. This truth historically has been the basic tenet of witchcraft and voodoo.

Some minds may have greater freedom of movement through the latticework than others: some minds may only be able to make small adjustments to their entropically determined course, veering just a few degrees in the desired direction and then only by great effort. Others may be more agile. A mind with the ability to move laterally, or sideways, through the lattice would perceive itself as having an ability to work miracles. "Sideways" here means in the direction of parallel states differing from the present state only by the desired characteristic, and neither distinctly "future" nor "past" to the present state.

Multiplication of loaves and fishes may be a case in point.[42] If by sheer act of imagination Jesus was able to transport his consciousness *and that of his followers* laterally to frames where the number of fish in the basket was greater, taking his audience's consciousnesses with him, the miracle is explained. The ability to move laterally, perpendicularly to the general entropic stream, and to take the minds of one's followers along for the ride, is consistent with divinity.

It was Christ himself who told us: "For verily I say unto you, That whosoever shall say unto this mountain, Be thou removed, and be thou cast into the sea; and shall not doubt in his heart, but shall believe that those things which he saith shall come to pass; he shall have whatsoever he saith. Therefore I say unto you, What things soever ye desire, when ye pray, believe that ye receive them, and ye shall have them."[43]

If we didn't know better, we might think Jesus Christ to be Wiccan! Certainly his awesome powers of manifesting are well documented in numerous instances.[44] Not the least of these is the time Christ withered a living fig tree in an instant.[45]

One is reminded of the game the object of which is to convert one word into a totally different word in a number of finite steps, changing only one letter at a time and always producing a valid word in the process. We change "spike" to "thorn" in five steps: spike, spire, shire, shore, shorn, thorn.

In this analogy, each letter change represents a quantum transition to a "contiguous" frame ("contiguous" here meaning the set of all words that differ from the given word by just one letter, where the entire lattice consists of all five-letter words). The mind constructs a route through the latticework to reach the desired destination.

The healing of illness by faith consists of transporting the patient's mind and that of his retinue of family, friends and acquaintances to a frame identical to the present frame except for the absence of the infirmity. If such a transition is accomplished rapidly by lateral or sideways travel through the latticework, the perception is that an instantaneous miracle has occurred—assuming the medical condition being cured was first diagnosed or at least observed. If the condition being cured was never diagnosed (persons praying for an unidentified lump to be diagnosed as non-malignant, followed by the desired negative diagnosis), there is no realization that intervention has even occurred.

Where a medical condition has not yet been diagnosed (as in the lump not yet biopsied), the conscious mind can be transported instantaneously to a frame consistent with any possible diagnosis. Using conventional parallel universe terminology, a "fusion" occurs with a universe representing a medical history consistent with the ultimate diagnosis.

Healing may be accomplished more gradually by travel on a diagonal line through the latticework. Here, there seems rapid improvement over a time, although the improvement may seem the result of explicable causes. ("The therapy worked.") In the "spontaneous" remission of serious illness, the perception is that the person is gradually improving.

The Intelligence of the universe operates at the quantum level. As perceived by the human mind, miracles always occur one quantum step at a time and are usually explicable in retrospect in terms of natural phenomena. Seemingly unrelated happenings simply cause events at hand to take an unexpected and previously improbable turn. The cause of this synergy or confluence of events from the past is rarely recognized.

One is reminded of the story of a preacher lecturing to a group of alcoholics on the power of prayer. The preacher asked if there were any present who did not believe in prayer. Several hands shot up. The speaker then succeeded in getting each member of his audience to admit that in time of deepest need he or she had in fact turned to prayer—each member of the audience but one, that is, who remained adamant.

Now turning all his attention to the one adamant nonbeliever, the preacher then said to him, "Surely there must have been a time in your life when you felt all hope was lost and you actually said a prayer." The man admitted that indeed once he had been on a hunting trip in the far north of Canada when he strayed away from his colleagues and from the campsite and became lost. "Darkness was falling. I had left my jacket and rifle back at the camp. The sun was setting and the temperature falling rapidly. I tried calling, shouting, but no one heard. I had no matches to even start a fire. I knew I was a long way from camp, but I had not the foggiest idea in which direction to go. A blizzard was setting in, and I felt I would die. So, yes, I admit I did in that one moment of weakness say a prayer."

"Well," retorted the preacher, "your prayer obviously worked. After all, you're here to tell us about it."

"Nope," said the man. "If an Indian on horseback hadn't ridden by at that very moment, I'd be dead now."

Witchcraft works. Voodoo works. So does prayer. Several double-blind studies prove the efficacy of prayer.

In an article entitled, "The power of prayer—divine intervention, quantum physics or a matter of mere quackery," appearing in the 24 October 2001 *Daily Telegraph* (London), Barbara Lantin tells of numerous double-blind experiments showing that ordinary Christian prayer helps the sick to heal. She quotes Steve Wright, associate professor to the faculty of health at St Martin's College, Lancaster, and an expert on healing:

> I am not talking about flaky new-age ideas but strong research. The person does not need to know that they are being prayed for, nor do they need to be known by the people doing the praying. And

there's no evidence that the more people who are involved, the more powerful the effect.

What seems to matter is having a sincere, focused, loving and compassionate intention for the wellbeing and healing of another. Knowing their name or having a picture seems to be an influential factor, perhaps because it provides a focus for the consciousness.[46]

And Richard Saltus writes in the *Boston Globe*:

[T]here's a fascinating study by Ralph C. Byrd, published in the Southern Medical Journal in 1988, that compared the outcomes of hospitalized cardiac patients, half of whom were prayed for by strangers, Christians who volunteered for the study. In this double-blind experiment—neither doctors nor patients knew who got the prayers—the prayed-for patients did significantly better: They had fewer heart attacks and contracted pneumonia less often, among other things.[47]

No formal studies have been run, to the author's knowledge, on the efficacy of witchcraft or voodoo.[48] But even Deutsch admits:

According to the 'Copenhagen interpretation', the equations of quantum theory apply only to unobserved aspects of physical reality. At moments of observation a different type of process takes over, *involving a direct interaction between human consciousness and subatomic physics.*[49]

The possibility of instantaneous movement of mind through lattice-work, without passing through any intervening frames, could explain even cataclysmic "miracles," Wiccan "magick" and "manifesting," and other psychic phenomena.

Telekinesis is the production of motion in objects by purely psychic means and without physical contact. Psychic teleportation is the instant transportation of some article to a distant location by purely psychic means. There is an instantaneous lateral movement of the subject's mind, and that of his retinue of family and associates privy to the event, to a frame identical to the starting point except for the absence of the moved object from its original position and the presence of that object in its new position. These minds can later rejoin a mainstream of minds moving through the superuniverse, but do so "swearing" that they witnessed a teleportation of some person or object.

The ability to instantaneously jump one's mind about the superuniverse opens possibilities of time travel as well. The concept is appealing that an immortal mind not locked in time need have no fear that the imminent destruction of our planet will in any way hinder his ability to visit any point on earth at any desired time with any set of buildings, places or persons imaginable. Astral projection is a case in point.

This prospect of multiple realities, unique to each individual, raises the possibility that the universe or God or superior forces may decide literally to teach some person a valuable lesson, to that end marching his mind through those frames that will result in his receiving the desired experiences. This is not deterministic or inconsistent with a free will. It's not an either-or proposition. We would hope that the more developed a mind becomes, the more freedom of movement that mind obtains. In this connection, a parent-child analogy is useful: that a parent may decide to give a child a particular learning experience does not negate that the child has a free will, nor does it mean that the child will not be given increased responsibilities in the future.

Yet if everyone is not to wander off in his own direction, leaving each individual totally alone in his or her own personal universe inhabited only by seemingly-sentient androids actually devoid of conscious minds, there must be some principle by which mind has affinity for mind, and minds tend to bunch together in groups for their peregrinations through the latticework.

Borrowing an analogy from Paul Davies,[50] imagine a large park with a fence around it and two gates on opposite sides. Suppose the park is situated in a busy metropolitan area such that people tend to enter through gate A, walk across to B, and exit. If we plot the tracks of visitors to the park over the course of a day, we may find several favored paths. Occasionally there will be a haphazard path. Perhaps a couple will walk together along the perimeter admiring the flowers. The majority of pedestrians will follow fairly closely to one of perhaps several trodden pathways through the park. Some may stray momentarily from one of these trodden pathways, only to return to that pathway later. Others may wander off the trodden path never to return.

Rupert Sheldrake and David Bohm have postulated the existence of "Morphogenetic Fields," or M-fields for short.[51] Their work is reminiscent of Carl Jung's well-known hypotheses of a "collective unconscious," of "primordial archetypes" and of "synchronicities."[52] It is fair to say that at the very least a large body of scientific data is accumulating to suggest that within a species, be it man, monkey or mouse, there is a strong affinity among minds.

One does not want to travel through the universe alone, even though the androids perceived by the lone voyager on his voyage would be indistinguishable from sentient beings.

Still, it does not strain the imagination to think that large groups of persons may depart from one of several possible "mainstreams" of minds moving through the superuniverse, forming their own separate "mainstream" or well-traveled path in the process. Victims of any massacre or holocaust may be an appropriate example for speculation: could forces of affinity binding minds together, or external forces, shunt each victim's consciousness on to a track through the latticework so as to spare that victim the indignity of being massacred? If so, for each member of the group the consciousness would have to branch off on the new course prior to certain knowledge that his fate had been sealed. Millions of Holocaust victims, for example, may happily exist on another track through the superuniverse, glad that Adolph Hitler never succeeded in taking office! Their reality would be every bit as accurate as our reality that Hitler indeed took office and massacred millions of Jews.

If we consider this line of reasoning, benevolent forces of nature or of God could have given the crazed despot mere matter in motion to massacre—persons whose consciousnesses were sent down happier paths of perception moments or years prior to the infliction of death.

If conscious minds previously on parallel tracks suddenly diverge, the now-absent mind is not noticed to be missing by his former traveling companions. The mind may have departed, but the body and brain remain and this non-sentient android continues to play out a movie-frame existence, devoid of consciousness but behaving exactly like a sentient being. The psychologist B. F. Skinner's materialistic laws of behavior apply, and this android's now-departed mind is never missed by his compatriots.

If conscious minds not previously on parallel tracks come together and travel through the same frames of the latticework of reality for a time, their convergence ("fusing" of parallel universes from the past, to use classical parallel-universes terminology) would in no way tip off the participants to the convergence of the paths. For in each participant's prior trek through different frames, the other participant has always appeared and seemed to move—an android uninhabited by a sentient mind until the convergence of the tracks occurs.

Nor can the fact of convergence or divergence be detected. It's as pointless to ask another human whether he is sentient as it is to ask a Cretan if he is truthful, since in either case the answer will always be "yes." The android will answer "yes" as readily as the sentient being.

There may be a restriction on convergence that precludes a convergence of those minds with memories that are grossly contradictory. Yet it is only our subjective perception of time that gives us this logical constraint. We imagine that divergence or "branching" into the future can contain no contradictions because the minds that so diverge are thereafter isolated from one another and cannot communicate. But when we reach into the past to find different minds with different histories merging into one present, it is tempting to assume a contradiction exists. Yet the "present" into which each of these minds converges must of necessity flow from each of their respective pasts by a logical series of quantum transitions.

How this works is not all that difficult. Assume a person—let's call him Jim—contracts a fatal disease and "dies." As far as this event is concerned, the population of the world may be divided into four groups. Group One consists of the set of all conscious persons who perceive Jim as dying (that is, all minds who learned or will at some future time learn of Jim's death from the illness). Group Two consists of conscious persons whose realities tell of Jim's recovery. Group Three consists of conscious persons whose realities fail to show Jim ever having fallen ill in the first place. Group Four consists of the remainder of humanity, the vast majority of minds who never heard and never will hear of Jim, and for whom his history is irrelevant and unknown.

We may assume Jim himself will be in Group Two or Group Three. Any other minds accompanying Jim on this perceptual path must of necessity also fall into Group Two or Group Three. The paths of conscious persons in Group One may from time to time briefly intersect with the paths of persons in Group Two, and this momentary reunion is permissible only so long as the subject of Jim does not come up in the conversation and so long as the ramifications of Jim's "death" or "cure" are not relevant to the particular interaction.

Since memories stored in the brain are quantum phenomena, it follows that in order for two minds to meet in the same frames in the latticework, they must manifest no grossly contradictory memories!

8

Conclusion

Children assume they will live forever. A child must be *taught* about death. Yet death is, after all, only what Wigner[53] discovers half the time when he opens the box containing the cat. Schrödinger's cat, on the other hand, has split into a parallel universe, blissfully unaware that it has "died."

Does the strong anthropic principle always favor that course of events in which the perceiver survives? Are we all immortal, each in his or her own frame of reference?

If our minds are immortal, how then (if at all) do we experience death? Do we, like Schrödinger's cat, perceive one continuous existence on this one planet earth? Is this one perceived, endless existence with ever-increasing mental mobility? Still alive and still housed in our own bodies? Or do we perceive a departure of mind from body and a sudden change in our physical state?

If there be any truth to the hypotheses of this book, "death" is perceived by the deceased as that point in time when the mind and body cease deteriorating and begin improving, either spontaneously or explicably through events such as "new" medical discoveries.

Does heaven exist right here on the planet earth, in more pleasant "editions" of the planet, while "hell" co-exists in parallel universes as less pleasant editions of this same planet?

Is death something that happens only to other persons, as they separate from us into other, parallel earths? Is death something that always eludes the observer, as we slip unawares into other versions of this very planet? Do each of us literally die a thousand deaths every day, unaware of each one?

Is reincarnation on this planet or on another plane the explanation for the seeming indestructibility of human consciousness?

The hypotheses presented have not been tested empirically. This book offers only a model. It is hoped this model is perhaps a more satisfying model in explanation of known quantum phenomena, such as the paradox of Schrödinger's Cat, than the widely-accepted but somehow repugnant concept of parallel dynamic universes.

Certainly the model is understandable, and may offer physicists, philosophers and theologians a springboard for discussion, while at the same time it offers philosophers and a framework for the reconciliation of observed "natural" and "supernatural" phenomena as well as a physical explanation of Wiccan manifesting and magick, as well as of Christian miracles.

Endnotes

1. Sir James Jeans, *The Mysterious Universe* (new revised ed.), New York: The Macmillan Company, 1932; Cambridge: The University Press, 1932), p. 186.

2. David Deutsch in *The Ghost in the Atom*, ed. Paul C. W. Davies and J. R. Brown (Cambridge: Cambridge University Press, 1986), p. 85.

3. P. C. W. Davies and J. R. Brown, ed., *The Ghost in the Atom* (Cambridge: Cambridge University Press, 1986).

4. P. C. W. Davies and J. R. Brown, ed., *ibid.,* pp. 35–36. (Emphasis added.)

5. David Deutsch in *The Ghost in the Atom*, ed. P. C. W. Davies and J. R. Brown (Cambridge: Cambridge University Press, 1986), p. 86.

6. Rushworth M. Kidder, "Living Proof of the Strange Quantum Ways," *Christian Science Monitor,* 15 June 1988, special pullout section p. B1.

7. "The Queerness of Quanta," *The Economist,* 7 January 1989, p. 85.

8. *Ibid.*

9. David Bohm, *Wholeness and the Implicate Order* (London: Routledge & Kegan Paul, 1981), p. 213.

10. A "googol" is the number 1 followed by a hundred zeroes. A "googleplex" is the number 1 followed by a googol of zeroes. The googol is a number far greater than the number of all electrons in the universe.

Both terms were originally introduced by Edward Kasner and James R. Newman in *Mathematics and the Imagination* (New York: Simon & Schuster, 1940; reprint, Redmond, Washington: Tempus Books of Microsoft Press, 1989; reprint Mineola, New York: Dover Publications, Inc., 2001), pp. 19–23.

11. Edward Kasner & James R. Newman, *Mathematics and the Imagination* (New York: Simon & Schuster, 1940; reprint, Redmond, Washington: Tempus Books of Microsoft Press, 1989; reprint Mineola, New York: Dover Publications, Inc., 2001), pp. 19-23.

12. James Gleick, "In a 'Random World,' He Collects Patterns," *New York Times,* 27 January 1987, City Final Ed., sec. C, p. 1.

13. N[eil] J[ames] A[lexander] Sloane, The Packing of Spheres; Mathematical Models and Industrial Applications," *Scientific American,* January 1984, vol. 250, p. 116.

14. J[ohn] H[orton] Conway & N[eil] J[ames] A[lexander] Sloane, *Sphere Packings, Lattices and Groups* (New York and London: Springer-Verlag, 1988). Chapter 30 of the book defines a remarkable Lie algebra of infinite dimensions, which would comprehend the problem of packing spheres in a space of an infinite number of dimensions.

15. H. Minkowski, "Space and Time," in *The Principle of Relativity* by H. A. Lorentz, A. Einstein, H. Minkowski & H. Weyl (London: Methuen and Company, Ltd., 1923; reprint, New York: Dover Publications, Inc., 1952), p. 75.

16. Henryk Skolimowski, "The Interactive Mind in the Participatory Universe," in Jean E. Charon, ed., *The Real and the Imaginary* (New York: Paragon House Publishers, 1987), pp. 69, 77.

17. A light year, of course, is the distance light travels in a year. At 186,284 miles per second, that comes to 5 trillion, 880 billion miles.

18. John Wheeler in *The Ghost in the Atom,* ed. P. C. W. Davies and J. R. Brown (Cambridge: Cambridge University Press, 1986), pp. 65, 67.

19. Deutsch even admits that "we do not know what consciousness is...." David Deutsch, *The Fabric of Reality* (New York: Penguin Putnam, Inc., 1997), p. 338.

20. Julian Jaynes, *The Origin of Consciousness in the Breakdown of the Bicameral Mind* (Boston: Houghton-Mifflin, Inc., 1976), p. 16.

21. Subhash Kak, *The Nature of Physical Reality,* Vol. 17, American University Studies, Series V. Philosophy (New York: Peter Lang, 1986), pp. 10-11.

22. Paul Davies, *God and the New Physics* (London: J. M. Dent & Sons Ltd., 1983). See also Douglas R. Hofstadter, *Gödel, Escher, Bach: An Eternal Golden Braid* (New York: Basic Books, Inc., 1979), pp. 708-710.

23. Karl Pribram, *Consciousness and the Brain* (New York: Plenum, 1976); Karl Pribram, *Languages of the Brain,* ed. G. Globus et al. (New York: Plenum, 1971).

24. Michael Talbot, *Beyond the Quantum* (New York: Macmillan Publishing Company, 1986), pp. 50-52.

25. Sir John Eccles, ed., *Mind and Brain* (New York: Paragon House Publishers, 1985).

26. Paul Davies, *Other Worlds* (New York: Simon & Schuster, 1980), pp. 137, 139.

27. David Deutsch, *The Fabric of Reality* (New York: Penguin Putnam, Inc., 1997), p. 277.

28. Michael Talbot, *Beyond the Quantum* (New York: Macmillan Publishing Company, 1986), p. 49.

29. Stephen Hawking, *A Brief History of Time* (New York: Bantam Books, 1988), p. 151.

30. See Fred Hoyle, *The Nature of the Universe,* rev. ed. (New York: Harper, 1960).

31. Fred Hoyle, *The Intelligent Universe* (New York: Holt, Rinehart & Winston, 1984), p. 161.

32. Jean E. Charon, *Complex Relativity* (New York: Paragon House Publishers, 1988).

33. Michael Talbot, *Beyond the Quantum* (New York: Macmillan Publishing Company, 1986), pp. 57, 70-71. *See also* Rupert Sheldrake, *New Science of Life* (Los Angeles: J. P. Tarcher, 1981).

34. Edgar Morin, "What Could be a Mind Able to Conceive a Brain Able to Produce a Mind?" in Jean E. Charon, ed., *The Real and the Imaginary* (New York: Paragon House Publishers, 1987), pp. 4, 5.

35. Michael Talbot, *Beyond the Quantum* (New York: Macmillan Publishing Company, 1986), p. 100.

36. *Ibid.* at 1.

37. "Fusion" of parallel universes from the past, to use High Everett's terminology.

38. Jorge Luis Borges, *Ficciones* (New York: Grove Press, Inc., 1962), pp. 97–100

39. New Line Cinema, 2000.

40. John Archibald Wheeler as quoted by Henryk Skolimowski, "The Interactive Mind in the Participatory Universe," in Jean E. Charon, ed., *The Real and the Imaginary* (New York: Paragon House Publishers, 1987), p. 69.

41. Fred Hoyle, *The Intelligent Universe* (New York: Holt, Rinehart & Winston, 1984), pp. 202-203.

42. Matthew 14:16-21; Mark 6:37-44; Luke 9:13-17; John 6:5-13.

43. Mark 11:23-24.

44. Matthew 21.

45. Matthew 21:19-20; Mark 11:13-20.

46. Steve Wright as quoted by Barbara Lantin in "The power of prayer—divine intervention, quantum physics or a matter of mere quackery," *Daily Telegraph* (London), 24 October 2001, p. 24.

47. Richard Saltus, "A Healthy Dose of Faith; Mind and Body," *Boston Globe,* 20 December 1998, Magazine p. 7.

48. But do see John Anthony West & Jan Gerhard Toonder, *The Case for Astrology* (London: Macdonald, 1970).

49. David Deutsch, *The Fabric of Reality* (New York: Penguin Putnam, Inc., 1997), p. 327. (Emphasis added.)

50. Paul Davies, *Other Worlds* (London: J. M. Dent & Sons Ltd.; New York: Simon & Schuster, 1980), p. 30.

51. Rupert Sheldrake & David Bohm, "Morphogenetic Fields and the Implicate Order," *Revision* 5, no. 2 (Fall 1982).

52. C. Jung (translation by R. F. C. Hull), *The Archetype and the Collective Unconscious* (New York: Pantheon Books, Inc., 1959).

53. Eugene Paul Wigner, the very real quantum physicist whose name is used in the hypothetical for the man who opens the box containing Schrödinger's imaginary cat—the cat itself being named after quantum physicist Erwin Schrödinger.

Glossary

A

action at a distance action upon an object with no physical connection. Action at a distance is instantaneous, *superluminal*. See also *causal order postulate*.

Andromeda Galaxy a large *galaxy* of about 300 billion stars. Visible in the constellation of Andromeda, it is one of the closest galaxies outside of our own galaxy, the Milky Way. It can be faintly seen with the naked eye, and lies at a distance of 2.381 million *light years*.

Ångström an extremely small unit of length, often used to measure the length of light waves. It is one ten-billionth of a meter, or one tenth of a nanometer.

anthropic principle in its weak form, the recognition that of all possible universes, in only a very few are the laws of physics so arranged as to be capable of supporting intelligent life. Accordingly, we ought not marvel that we are in one of the few possible places capable of supporting life. This is also known as the *weak anthropic principle*. See also *strong anthropic principle*.

Aspect experiment Alain Aspect, of l'Institut d'Optique Theorique et Appliquée in Orsay, France, conducted the definitive experiment with *polarized* light that compels the conclusion that *action at a distance* is possible and causation may relate backwards in time. See also *Causal Order Postulate*.

B

Bell's Theorem this mathematical theorem postulates that atomic particles or *photons* having a common origin (for example, a pair of *photons* thrown out simultaneously by the same atom) remain forever connected to one another across time and space.

bicameral mind Julian Jaynes's theory that the human mind is compartmentalized, with an "executive part" and a "follower part." Jaynes then postulated that consciousness somehow evolved out of the breakdown of this bicameral mind.

Big Bang hypothesis The theory that the universe started with a big bang at a definite instant between 13 and 20 billion years ago, when all matter in the universe suddenly exploded into being from an infinitesimal point. This theory is generally accepted today, largely as the result of the discovery in 1963 by Arno Penzias and Robert Wilson of Bell Laboratories of what can best be explained as the radio echoes of the Big Bang reverberating throughout the universe. See also *steady-state theory*.

C

Causal Order Postulate the postulate that for event A to cause event B, event A must occur earlier in time than event B. This postulate has been disproven by the *Aspect experiment*. It is now settled in quantum physics that causation can move backwards in time.

contiguous touching.

Copenhagen Interpretation a set of rules of quantum physics proposed in the 1920s by Danish scientist Niels Bohr. It includes the *Heisenberg Principle of Uncertainty,* and adds that light or electromagnetic radiation may behave as a wave or as a particle but not as both at the same time. Measuring anything at the atomic level changes that which is measured.

corpuscular existing in minute particles. The corpuscular theory of light that posits that light consists of minute particles, as opposed to the wave theory of light. Both theories, it appears, are true. See *two-slit experiment.*

cosmological constant the mathematical factor that determines whether the universe is expanding and will expand forever, is expanding now but eventually will contract back to a single point, or is expanding now but eventually will slow down without ever contracting.

cosmology the branch of astronomy that studies the universe taken as a whole.

D

dynamic moving, in motion, as opposed to *static.*

E

energy state as used here, a still picture of the universe, a particular condition of the universe, an arrangement of atomic particles constituting the universe. If one electron on just one atom moves just one iota, the still picture of that universe is different and constitutes a different energy state.

entropy a measure of the unavailable heat in any closed system (here, the entire universe). See *Second Law of Thermodynamics.*

F

fourth dimension time, according to Einstein. Space appears to consist of three dimensions—in common parlance, length, width, and depth. For example, three mutually perpendicular lines can be placed through a single point, but not a fourth. Einstein felt that time was a fourth dimension. We now know that there are far more than four dimensions.

G

galaxy a collection of hundreds of billions of stars held together by mutual gravitational attraction. Galaxies are often flat and disc-shaped, with spiral arms of stars extending from the center.

gluon a subatomic particle. Together with *quarks*, gluons are the building blocks out of which many atomic particles, including protons and neutrons, are constituted.

googol the number 1 followed by a hundred zeroes. The googol is a number far greater than the number of all electrons in the universe. The term was originally introduced by Edward Kasner and James R. Newman.

googolplex the number 1 followed by a *googol* of zeroes. The terms *googol* and googolplex were originally introduced by Edward Kasner and James R. Newman.

gravitational lens An extremely heavy object such as a *galaxy* whose gravitational field bends light coming from more distant sources behind it in the same line of sight, with the effect of making those more distant objects visible. The objects, however, appear in double images or multiple images. Thus, the same distant *quasar* can be seen as separate images, perhaps one above the intervening *galaxy*, another below the intervening galaxy, and perhaps several more off to one side or another.

H

Heisenberg Principle of Uncertainty proposed by Werner Heisenberg in 1927, a photon or atomic particle may have position or it may have momentum, but it may not in any true sense of the word have both. Measurement of one (position or momentum) necessarily destroys or alters the other.

hexagon a regular, two-dimensional polygon having six sides.

hyperface the face of a hyperpolyhedron. This "face" would have more than two dimensions. For example, two universes existing in hyperspace could touch at all points in the three-dimensional space of each of the universes.

hyperpolyhedron a *polyhedron* existing in four or more dimensions. A hyperpolyhedron is to a *polyhedron* what a *polyhedron* is to a *polygon*.

hyperspace space containing more than three physical dimensions.

hypersphere a sphere existing in four or more dimensions. A hypersphere is to a sphere what a sphere is to a circle.

J

jiffy the smallest imaginable quantum unit of time, 10^{-43} seconds, being that fraction of a second represented by the number 1 over the number 10 followed by 42 zeros. There are more jiffies in a single second than there are seconds in all the time since the beginning of the universe.

L

lattice here used to indicate a regular geometric arrangement in hyperspace of all imaginable three-dimensional universes.

light, speed of *see speed of light.*

light year a unit of distance, not time, being the distance light travels in one year going at the *speed of light.* Roughly 5 trillion 880 billion (5,880,000,000) miles. For comparison, the Moon is only 1.3 light seconds away. It takes light from the Moon just 1.3 seconds to reach the earth. The Sun is 8.2 light minutes away. The nearest star (other than our Sun) is 4.22 light years away. The nearest *galaxy* (other than our own Milky Way) is the Large Magellanic Cloud, visible from the Southern Hemisphere. It is 163,080 light years away. The *Andromeda Galaxy* is 2,381,000 light years away. When you look skyward and see the *Andromeda Galaxy*, you see it as it was 2.38 million years ago. Yet the *Andromeda Galaxy* is one of the nearer galaxies! More distant galaxies are billions of light years distant from earth. We see them as they were much earlier in the evolution of the universe, for as we look out in space we look backwards in time.

M

materialism the belief that nothing exists but matter. This atheistic philosophy rejects the existence of anything spiritual, has great difficulty explaining consciousness, and is in an absolute state of denial of miracles, occult phenomena and the paranormal. This is the operative philosophy of many scientists.

multiverse a term in conventional *quantum physics* describing the collection of all parallel universes. Hugh Everett's "many worlds" hypothesis posits the existence of a multiverse. That multiverse, however, consists of a multiplicity of *dynamic* universes. Compare with *superuniverse.*

N

noncontiguous said of two things not directly touching one another.

P

photon a particle of light under the *corpuscular* theory of light.

phylogeny history of the evolution of the species.

polarization the direction, vertical or horizontal (or anything in between), in which light waves are undulating. It is useful to think of waves passing along a length of rope being shaken. The rope can be shaken vertically, in which case the waves along the rope have vertical polarization (and if the rope passes through a fence with vertical slats, this "polarizing filter" will permit the vertical waves to pass right through. But if the rope is shaken horizontally, in which case the waves have horizontal polarization, the fence will not permit them to pass. All *photons* are polarized.

polygon A two-dimensional geometric figure existing in two-dimensional space, having several "sides" in the form of one-dimensional straight lines. Contiguous polygons touch by sharing a one-dimensional side with an adjacent polygon.

polyhedron A three-dimensional geometric solid existing in three-dimensional space, having several "faces" in the form of two-dimensional sides. Contiguous polyhedra touch by sharing a two-dimensional face with an adjacent polyhedron.

postulate an assumed truth underlying any hypothesis.

Q

quantum the smallest possible unit (of energy, time, gravity, etc.). These are not arbitrary units set by limitations on our measuring methods, but it is inherent in the universe itself that all events at the sub-atomic level occur in little jerks or jumps called quanta.

quantum physics the study of matter at the subatomic level.

quantum theory the postulate of quantum physics that all events at the subatomic occur in little jerks or jumps called quanta.

quantum transition a *quantum* jump of any particle in the universe. Here used to distinguish two *static universes* that differ from one another by one and only one *quantum* jump of one and only one electron, photon or subatomic particle.

quark a subatomic particle. Together with *gluons*, quarks are the building blocks out of which many atomic particles, including protons and neutrons, are constituted.

quasar quasi-stellar radio source. These objects are extremely bright. Farther away than most *galaxies,* these are the most distant and the brightest objects in the universe. They may be *galaxies* in collision, or *galaxies* being eaten by a black hole.

R

rhombic dodecahedron a geometric solid consisting of twelve rhombic (diamond-shaped) faces. Rhombic dodecahedra nest or pack perfectly (as do cubes), with no unused space between them.

S

Schrödinger's Cat an imaginary experiment, never actually carried out, in which a cat is placed in a box along with a vial of poison. A hammer trips and breaks the vial or does not trip and does not release the poison depending on a random quantum event. Quantum physics requires the cat to go into two superimposed states, one of being half dead and the other of being half alive. Only when the box is opened does reality "collapse in" on the events. (In the classic description of the experiment, the box is opened by "Wigner's friend.")

Second Law of Thermodynamics proposed by Rudolf Julius Emmanuel Clausius in 1857, the theory posits that heat or energy moves from hot objects to colder places, and that eventually any closed system will reach thermal equilibrium with everything at the same temperature. Since heat can accomplish work only when it moves from a warm place to a cooler place, once thermal equilibrium is reached all the heat in the closed system is still present but now unavailable to accomplish any work. Applied to the universe as a whole, the law suggests that the universe is slowly winding down. See also *entropy*.

sentient having consciousness, awareness.

solipsism the philosophical theory that the self is the only thing that really exists, all else is a product of your imagination, and the universe exists only in your mind.

spacetime as Hermann Minkowski said of Einstein's theories, "Henceforth space by itself, and time by itself, are doomed to fade away into mere shadows, and only a kind of union of the two will preserve an independent reality."

speed of light the velocity at which light travels, 186,284 miles per second (299,776 kilometers per second). Einstein "proved" that nothing can travel faster than light, but the *Aspect experiment* showed that some *superluminal* effects are possible. See also *action at a distance*.

sphere packing the challenge of packing spheres (*e.g.*, ping-pong balls or oranges) into a given space so as to get the maximum number of spheres into that space.

static stationary, not moving, still. As opposed to *dynamic*.

static universe An entire universe frozen in time—completely still, unchanging for all eternity.

steady-state theory the now largely discredited *uniformitarian* theory, advanced by Fred Hoyle, Hermann Bondi and Thomas Gold in 1948, that the universe was not created but has always been in existence without beginning or end, and that the universe looks no different now than it looked millions, billions or even trillions of years ago. This theory tries to explain away the unquestioned fact that the universe is expanding by positing that new matter is continuously and spontaneously being created out of nothingness to fill the voids resulting from the expansion. The demise of this theory came with the discovery in 1963 by Arno Penzias and Robert Wilson of Bell Laboratories of what can best be explained as the radio echoes of the Big Bang reverberating throughout the universe. See also *Big-bang hypothesis*.

strong anthropic principle less firmly established than the *weak anthropic principle,* the strong anthropic principle postulates that events must unfold so as to preserve the observer. This seems a logical conclusion of *Schrödinger's Cat*.

superluminal faster than the *speed of light*.

superposition here used to indicate two *static universes* that differ by only one *quantum transition,* superimposed on one another (contiguous in the three physical dimensions).

superuniverse the grand universe composed of all imaginable parallel universes. It exists in *hyperspace*. The superuniverse posited by the author differs from the *multiverse* of conventional quantum physics in that here each parallel universe is absolutely still, static, frozen, not moving and dynamic.

synapse in the brain, that junction in a neural pathway between two neurons. It is where thinking occurs.

T

transfinite greater than infinity. Infinity squared is still just infinity. Infinity to the power *n*, where *n* is any real number, is still just infinity. But infinity to the power of infinity is transfinite. For example, all possible whole numbers constitute an infinite set. Any segment of that infinite set (*e.g.,* all whole numbers from 20,000 to 25,000) is, however, a finite set. But any segment of a transfinite set, however small, is still an infinite set.

truncated octahedron a geometric solid consisting of fourteen faces: six squares and eight hexagons. Truncated octahedra nest or pack perfectly (as do cubes), with no unused space between them.

two-slit experiment an experiment designed to determine if light is *corpuscular* or composed of waves. Light, it appears, has multiple personalities, sometimes behaving as particles, other times as waves.

U

uniformitarianism a theory associated with Sir Charles Lyall, that geological processes have always operated uniformly over the ages and the world has always been much as we see it today. The cosmological equivalent of such thinking is the *steady-state theory*.

Urantia Book a spiritualistic book published in 1955 describing the universe in metaphysical terms and containing purported messages from extraterrestrials. The Urantia Book has no established basis in physical science. The author of the present book has borrowed the term *superuniverse* from *The Urantia Book,* but does not by so doing indicate any intent to endorse *The Urantia Book.*

W

weak anthropic principle the recognition that of all possible universes, in only a very few are the laws of physics so arranged as to be capable of supporting intelligent life. Accordingly, we ought not marvel that we live in one of the few possible places capable of supporting life, for we could not expect to be living elsewhere. See also *strong anthropic principle*.

Wigner's friend named after Eugene Paul Wigner, a very real quantum physicist, this is the man who opens the box containing *Schrödinger's (imaginary) cat*—the cat itself being named after quantum physicist Erwin Schrödinger.

About the Cover Picture

The Witch Head Nebula image by Gary Stevens. This object is at a distance of about a thousand light years (5 quadrillion, 880 trillion miles). The astronomical catalogue number of the Witch Head Nebula is IC 2118, and it is located in the constellation of Eridanus.

About the Author

M. R. Franks, associate professor of law at Southern University, Baton Rouge, Louisiana. Formerly professeur associé de droit at l'Université de Cergy-Pontoise, Paris, France. The author, a life member of the Royal Astronomical Society of Canada, has belonged to that organization since 1957. His interest in quantum physics and cosmology dates back to his childhood. A licensed airline transport pilot as well, Professor Franks holds his Bachelor of Science and Juris Doctor degrees from the University of Memphis.

M. R. Franks
Post Office Box 281
Baton Rouge, Louisiana
USA 70821-0281
Telephone (800) 227-5345
mfranks@manyuniverses.com

Index

0-595-29472-3

Printed in the United States
103825LV00010B/120/A